Published by: TAG Books
                        P.O. Box 111
                        Independence OR 97351

Distributed by: Wade Martin's Bonanza Distribution
                         Bend, OR 97701

Cover Design and Artwork by Sheila Somerville

Printed in the United States

Second Edition

Copyright 1993 - Gary D. Trump

ISBN: 1-884366-00-7

Other books in the Uncle Bud series:

Sweet Memories

Tom, Pete, Luther and Joe all come into the restaurant every morning. We have coffee and shoot the breeze a while. They're good friends. They must be — we all have the same enemies.

All my life I've heard people say "The early bird catches the worm." Well, that's true enough, I guess, but how come nobody looks at it from the worm's point of view?

Martha always forgives me. I can't count the number of times I've blundered and fouled up — but she can.

Have you ever gone to the doctor and said "It hurts right here" and he sort of glances at the spot and says "That doesn't bother me."? Well of course it doesn't bother you, you idiot, it bothers me. Why do you think I brought it up? Idle curiosity to see if the rest of the world hurts in the same place?

Actually, I have to say that most of us live longer because of doctors, and I'm glad they don't have to admit their mistakes. It would be really depressing to walk through a cemetery and see all of those headstones with "Oops!" chiseled on them.

It's hard to forget your first day in the Army. I guess the military thinks that ears are for holding up hats — at least that's how it worked out for me. And considering the size of the shirts they gave me, I didn't really need pants. They issued 'em to me anyway. It turned out they were a little loose around the armpits.

Tom, Pete, Joe and Luther were in here yesterday morning for coffee, as usual. We were talking politics and Luther was saying something on the subject.

Young Warren Teal was finishing his breakfast, and as he was paying at the register, he looked over at Luther and said "Go ahead and tell 'em all you know, Luther. It'll only take a minute."

Luther sipped his coffee and gently set down his mug before looking over at Warren. "And if they've got a minute and five seconds, I'll tell 'em what we both know."

The guy down the road has a wife, five kids and a dog the size of a yearling steer. Early every morning he would walk the dog past my house, and let the critter do his duty in my yard. I got into an argument with this fella about it. Some hard words were said, and I felt kind of guilty about it afterward. At Christmas time I told him how sorry

I was and, just to show there were no hard feelings, I gave each of the five kids a nice new drum.

We'd never be so stupid as to choose a car or a house by the light of the moon ... a spouse, sure, but never a car or a house.

Old George Graines was a great storyteller, and he liked to tell of a funeral that took place back when he was a boy. It seems that there was a fellow named Casper Jenks who had a wife that was a real shrew. She devoted her life to making Casper as miserable as she knew how. Casper was a little, timid sort of guy and wouldn't put up much of a fight. I don't recall the wife's name, but anyhow one day she died. This was back in the days when people just laid the body out at home, got it dressed for the occasion, put it in a coffin and held a service at the house. Then they loaded the box into a wagon and headed for the graveyard.

Well, all this came to pass, and when they got to the cemetery, the pallbearers took the coffin out of the wagon and started for the grave. But something went wrong. On the way in, they ran into a gatepost and dropped the box. The lid flew off and the old lady rolled out on the ground — and woke up. She wasn't dead after all. She went on to devil old Casper for five more years.

Well, she died again and everybody had to do it all over. Only this time, when the pallbearers went to carry the coffin through the cemetery gate, they found Casper guiding them through.

"Steady boys," he said, as if they were carrying dynamite. "Steady now ... mind that post ... steady ..."

There was a young fella that used to come in here for breakfast every morning, and he spent most of his time telling anyone who'd listen about his boss. "He's an idiot," the kid would say. "You never saw such a fool."

Finally, Joe got tired of listening to it. "Y'know, Jerry," Joe said, "I'm pretty well acquainted with both you and your boss, and I have to agree with you."

Jerry puffed up a little more. "You do?" he asked. He looked over at Tom, Pete and Luther, who sat drinking their coffee and waiting for the other shoe to drop. "See what I mean?" the kid said. "He knows."

"I not only know," smiled Joe, "I can prove it."

"You can?"

"Anybody who'd keep you on the payroll has got to be a fool."

I've got a little office in the back, and Martha is always coming in and straightening up my desk. How can I find anything if it's all where it's supposed to be?

Being 'average' isn't so hot when you consider it's only the best of the worst and the worst of the best.

LeRoy, who's a few cards short of a full deck anyhow, was pulling a chain behind him the other day. Some of the fellas were laughing about it, and one of 'em said "LeRoy how come you're pulling a chain down the street?" Leroy stopped and looked at him a while, then he raised an eyebrow and said "you ever try pushin' one?"

When I first walked into this place, I got to talking to the guy behind the counter who turned out to be the owner. He told me the cafe was for sale.

"Not so long ago I was doing fine," he said, sadly. "I was making money, had some put away ... everything was going pretty well."

"Then you lost everything, right?" I asked.

"Well," he said, "I fell in with a fast crowd. Booze, women, gambling ... mostly it was the gambling."

"And you lost it all," I said.

He looked at me like I was crazy. "Are you kidding?" he laughed. "I won. I won money hand over fist." He slowly shook his head. "So I bought this stupid cafe. Then I lost everything."

Politicians do serve a useful purpose. It's always good to have someone the rest of us can point to and realize we're not so bad after all.

Our kids made a habit of showing up at the door with some critter, and the first words out of their mouths were always "It followed me home. Can I keep it?" Now as far as the critter is concerned, it could have been anything from a baby bunny to a bull elephant. And in many cases, it followed them home at the end of a rope, kickin' and fightin' every step of the way. We told the kids, "No more. From now on, you don't carry or drag one more beast into this house."

Then Kyle showed up with a kitten, and by gosh, it really did follow him home. That kitten was just a little ball of grey fur, no bigger 'n a minute, and almost starved.

Today, he's an eighteen pound Manx and asleep on the sofa as I write this. He long ago elected himself lord of the manor and, even though the kids are grown and gone, he still rules supreme. Not too long ago Kyle came by for a visit, and we got to talking about that cat.

"You know, Dad," he said, "I was riding my

6

bike about a half-mile from the house when I heard this little "meow" back in the brush. When I found that little kitten, I felt so sorry for him — he was almost done in. I jumped on my bike and rode down to the store and bought a half-pint of milk. When I got back, he was still there, and I poured a little milk in my hand and let him drink. I remembered what you and Mom had said, so I started for home with him trying to keep up. He was so little, he couldn't go very fast, and so starved, I had to stop every few steps so he could rest and have some more milk. It's true. He did follow me home, but we had to go real, real slow."

Well, his majesty just opened one eye, looked at me, licked his paw, and scrubbed an ear before he went back to sleep. It was only a half-mile from the poorhouse to the palace.

What a man does in public won't tell you too much about him. If you could see what he does when he thinks nobody is looking, it would tell you a lot more.

It's not hard to get the lion to lie down with the lambs — of course, you do have to add more lambs from time to time.

It seems to me that every customer who walks in the door is interesting in his or her own way. Not likeable necessarily, but interesting.

Wilber Shoop was in a while back, and he had a shiner you wouldn't believe.

"Wilber," I said, "who gave you the black eye?"

"My wife," he muttered.

"Your wife? I thought she was out of town visiting her mother."

"So did I."

It seems like we're always washing windows and mirrors around here. Rather than buy the ready made stuff, I just put three cups of ammonia and one cup of white vinegar in a gallon jug and fill it with water. I add a few drops of glycerin (you can get it at the drugstore) to give the glass a nice shine. To make it look like the well-known national brand, I add a little blue food coloring. By the way, wadded up newspaper works best for wiping off windows and mirrors.

Old Bill Richey was quite a man. He made a fortune in farming and selling farm equipment. He worked all his life, and he had the calluses to prove it. His son and daughter-in-law stick their pinky fingers up when they're drinking their tea, and their noses up when they're not. But old Bill was common as dirt.

One summer, on the hottest day of the year, I came across Bill alongside the road. He was changing a flat tire. His daughter-in-law, Ethel, was sitting in the car because there wasn't a tree or any other shade for a mile or more.

I pulled over. "Bill, let me give you a hand there," I said.

Bill was gettin' up there in years and was already wringing wet, so he pulled an old red bandanna out of his back pocket, mopped his face and said, "Don't mind if I do."

"Sure a hot one today, isn't it?" I said, as I started to work.

"Enough to make the sweat roll," old Bill agreed.

Ethel was sitting right there with the window rolled down. "Father Richey," she said, not wanting a commoner like me to get the wrong idea, "horses sweat. Men perspire."

Bill's eyes kind of narrowed as he looked down at her. "What do ladies do then?"

She kind of sniffed and lifted her head a little higher. "Ladies ... glow."

Bill leaned over and gave her a long look. "Yer glowin' like a horse, Ethel."

The guy who's rich enough not to worry about losing his golf ball is usually so old he can't hit it far enough to lose it.

Now the Grahams weren't part of the upper crust, but they sure wanted to be. One time they invited the Richeys over for dinner. How old Bill happened to go along, I never heard, but I'd guess that he wasn't in a real good humor by the time the meal was done.

The Grahams had a daughter who played classical music on the piano. That would be alright I guess, but I heard her play once, and it sounded like tomcats fighting in a tinware shop. Anyhow, the girl is playing and Mrs. Graham kind of sidles up to old Bill and says "She plays beautifully, doesn't she?"

"What?" asked Bill.

"I said she plays --"

"Eh?" said Bill, cupping a hand to his ear.

"I said --"

"I can't hear you," yelled Bill, "what with that infernal racket comin' from that damned piano."

It's been my experience that a man doesn't often complain with his mouth full.

Like a GI will do when he's home on leave, I'd go around and revisit the places I enjoyed as a kid. It was late in the spring, and I parked the car and walked down to the ol' swimmin' hole. The first thing I saw, there at the edge of the water, was an old tin washtub that I'd tried to use as a boat ten years before. The next thing I saw was Louise Richey's head sticking out of the water.

"Get out of here," she yelled.

Well, I went to high school with Louise, and with her family being wealthy and mine being poor, she always cruised by me like a battleship passing a barge. I don't recall that she ever said a civil word to me. Anyhow, I looked over and saw her clothes draped over a bush a few feet away. Louise was skinny-dippin' in the ol' swimmin' hole.

"You get out of here right now!"

Well a gentleman would have left, no doubt about it, and I was getting around to it; but being in the mood to reminisce, I was thinking about all the times she was mean to me and the other kids. I guess the water was a little cold, because after a while, Louise made her way over to that old washtub and picked it up, holding it out in front of herself as she walked toward her clothes.

When she was about ten feet away, she kind of hissed and her eyes shot sparks, and she said, "I bet you think you're pretty smart."

I smoked at the time, so I lit one up and leaned back against a tree. "Louise," I said, I bet you think there's still a bottom in that old tub."

Some people will sacrifice anything to become a success. I can't say I envy them a whole lot. Usually, after they've made it, they look around and realize that the rest of their life is unbelievably screwed up.

There was a letter came to the post office a while back addressed only to "The Worst Cook in the State" with our city and zip code. Now people

12

are entitled to their opinions, but I'm never gonna forgive that mailman for walking right into the cafe and handing it to me.

Everybody around here knows that old McTavish was tight with a dollar. There's a story making the rounds that he thought he'd rest more comfortably if he had a little cash with him when he was buried. He probably thought he'd need it for bribes.

Anyway, McTavish told his lawyer that if he'd put a thousand dollars in the coffin at the funeral then McTavish would leave him twice that amount in his will. McTavish wasn't too trusting, I guess, so he went around and told his doctor and minister the same thing. They all agreed to do as he asked.

Well, time passed and finally old McTavish croaked. He was laid out, talked about and planted, all with due ceremony, and the three men met at the lawyer's office for the reading of the will.

The preacher seemed kind of upset and, when asked about it, squirmed a good deal and then finally spoke up. "I only put five hundred dollars in the coffin with McTavish," he confessed. "We've had some extra large expenses lately, and it seemed such a waste."

"I saw what you did," the doctor said. "It seemed to me that if you could do it, I could too, so I only put in five hundred dollars myself."

"You're both a couple of cheapskates!" the lawyer yelled. "When I saw what you two had done, I took the cash and wrote a check for the entire amount."

He probably felt pretty good about it, too, until a few days later when the undertaker cashed the check.

A meeting should never last more than five minutes. This is because all the really important business is taken care of out in the hallway anyhow.

It seems kind of odd that the world's most important job, that of being a parent, is open to the people with the least qualifications. I guess that's why so many people buy books written by some doctor on how to raise children. Those doctors usually go to great lengths telling parents how to let kids have their own way.

Jean has worked here several years now and everybody likes her. She's kind of an extra "mom" to the college kids I hire to wait tables, and the customers think she's great. She almost didn't make it through her first day, though.

When she applied for the job, she was really nervous. She was divorced with a couple of little

girls to support, and I could tell she really needed the job. That first morning she rushed around trying to do more than her share and get everything done at once.

The breakfast rush was over, and I was working in the kitchen getting some things ready for lunch. I looked out and there was Jean, picking up dirty dishes until she had a stack she couldn't see over. I had a sneaking suspicion what was coming, but I just shook my head and went back to work. I had my back to the door when I heard it open.

You know there's that certain sound that a stack of dishes make just before they decide to commit mass suicide? I kind of braced myself, and the crash was enormous. Then it got real quiet.

"Just put 'em down anywhere, Jean," I said, in a friendly, conversational tone. If anything, it got quieter, but I didn't turn around. I kept on working and, I've got to admit, I was wondering if I wasn't alone by that time.

Then I heard a "clink" of glass. Then another and another and pretty soon a broom went to work. I won't say Jean hasn't dropped anything since, but I will say I'm glad I didn't turn around.

Hair spray is good for taking out ink stains from pens or felt tip markers. It works well for taking those black scuff marks off shoes, too.

I've never been much of a 'joiner'. It seems to me that Groucho Marx had it right when he said "I refuse to become a member of any organization that would consider having someone like me as a member."

When I came of age, my Dad took me aside and warned me about a saloon and dancehall named Curly's. Of course, I already knew about it. It was famous for its wild parties and wilder women.

"You'll see things in there you shouldn't see," Dad told me. Well, he was right about that. The first thing I saw when I walked in the door was Dad.

We're doomed. Civilization as we know it is about to disappear from the earth. You may think I don't know what I'm talking about, but I have concrete evidence to support my theory.

Every morning these old duffers come in here for their morning coffee and spend about half their time talking about the local high school. I've been paying close attention, and they all agree that forty or fifty years ago, when they were in school, the boys were all twice as tall, fast, athletic, handsome and intelligent as those today. Every girl was gorgeous beyond belief and could have been a brain surgeon had she not elected to marry that fool and raise a bunch of dopey kids.

17

Yes, the eyewitnesses are here having coffee every morning. From what they say, there can be only one conclusion. At its current rate of decline, it can only be a few generations before the human race crawls back into the slimy sea and leaves the land to be retaken by the dinosaur and wooly mammoth.

There's always somebody stopping by here on their way to the tennis courts out at the club. Sometimes they leave a tennis ball behind. Now a tennis ball has its uses.

I've cut a hole in one and used it to cover the trailer ball on my pickup to keep it from rusting. If you have a broken light bulb, you can push a tennis ball up against what's left of the bulb and unscrew it from the socket. When you have large items to put in the washer, like the dirty aprons we have around here or, say bedsheets, just toss a couple of tennis balls into the machine along with the load. The agitator bats them around and things come out cleaner.

Always remember the day of your wife's birthday. Always forget the year.

I know it's not the "in" thing these days to talk about fried foods, but I have to say I've always been a big fan of cast iron cookware. As a kid in cow camp, we had a cook who could make biscuits in an old cast iron dutch oven that you wouldn't believe. Light? Pardner, when we sat down to eat, if some damn fool left the lid off the oven, those biscuits would float away. We had to keep a shotgun handy to get 'em down if somebody slipped up.

I know cast iron is heavy and clumsy to work with, but there's nothing like that steady, even heat for cooking food to a turn. I like to "season" my pans by wiping them down with vegetable shortening and baking them in an oven at low heat (250-300 degrees) for about an hour and a half. Every so often I pull them out and wipe them down with a paper towel soaked in shortening. When they're done, I polish them up with a paper towel or newspaper. A newspaper you say? Well, that's what I do. I can't recommend it to others, though, because somebody's sure to use a dirty hunk of newspaper and then sue me because they got sick.

If you happen to have some deep frying to do, reach for that old cast iron skillet. Not only will it do a fine job, it will also "season" itself in the process. That's another thing about good cast iron skillets. The more they're used, the better they work. I've had mine for years, and I wouldn't trade 'em for any other cookware you could mention.

A lot of dutch ovens on the market these days have the rounded lid. I guess that's alright for the stove top or oven, but mine is one of the old style.

It's got three little short legs and a flat lid with a lip around the edge so you can pile on live coals from the campfire. It goes with me whenever I go camping. Sure, it's good for bread or biscuits, but it can also make soups and stews that are out of this world. Beans and hamhocks? Oh, Momma, the lost is found.

The last thing I'll say on the subject is that a lot of old timers and some darn good cooks today rarely wash their cast iron cookware. Again, I don't recommend that because somebody might get sick, but the theory is that washing the pan washes out the "seasoning." If grease was used to cook with and nothing has stuck to the cooking surface (and it usually hasn't to a well-seasoned pan), they just wipe it out with a piece of clean newspaper or paper towel.

There's a restaurant down the street that employs twice as many people as I do. Fortunately, they only have half as many working.

Elmer swears he was forced into being a drunk. (He says his annual income isn't high enough for him to be an alcoholic.) Anyhow, he claims he was walking down a dark street one night when a man stepped out of an alley armed with a pistol. Elmer threw up his hands, sure he was about to be robbed.

"Here," said the assailant, thrusting a paper bag into Elmer's arms. "Drink this."

Inside, Elmer found a fruit jar full of liquid. He took a swallow. "Ugh!" he said. "This is just about the worst moonshine I ever tasted."

"It is, isn't it?" said the man, as he held out the pistol to Elmer. "Now, you hold the gun and make me take a drink."

I had a cousin who was a professional window washer. He was working on the sixth floor of an office building one day when he fell. The only thing that saved him was he landed on the roof of a parked car. At the emergency room, one of the nurses asked what he did for a living.

"Well, I used to be a window washer," he said.

"Oh," she replied, "when did you quit?"

"As near as I can recall, it was around the third floor."

Luther comes in every morning for coffee, but unlike the other fellas, Luther usually has a little breakfast, too. Luther's a bachelor and, while he doesn't mind cooking at other times, he won't do it in the morning.

"Never could get the hang of cookin' with my eyes closed," he says.

Luther was raised in Idaho and claims he was married once. "She was nice enough," Luther says, "but she had a mother that'd make an Army drill sergeant look like a choir boy." Shaking his head, he'll say, "She was a brutal woman. Just brutal."

"Once," says Luther, "not long after Clara and me was married, I got to the point where I didn't think I could take it no longer. Her mother was over to our house three times ever' day and at least half of ever' night. I'd sooner have Hitler as a houseguest.

"It was fall, and I announced I was goin' deer huntin'. It was a stupid mistake to let the word out ahead of time like that. But, at first, it seemed like a good idea. Clara had never been deer huntin' before, and she said she'd like to go along. *Well, I thought to myself, here's a chance for me an' Clara to get away and spend a week all by ourselves.*

"I had a favorite campin' spot away back in the mountains. It was so far back in the brush, you had to pipe in your own sunshine. Now Clara's mother had all the instincts of a bloodhound, even though I always thought she favored a bulldog as far as looks are concerned. Anyhow, I knew she'd have a hard time findin' us where we were headed.

"Well, the great day came. I'd packed up the old pickup the night before, and it was just comin' daylight when we walked out of the house. I opened the door to the truck and durn near fainted when I saw Clara's mother sittin' in there.

'*After you went to bed last night,*' Clara said, '*Mother decided she'd like to come along. You don't mind do you, sweetie?*'

"Mind? I just stood there and got sick to my stomach. It was all I could do to keep from tossin' my waffles right on the spot. Finally, I got in and we started out. This had turned out to be a real bad idea.

"While Clara's mother was givin' me directions and tellin' me how to drive, I was thinkin' about how I was gonna get out of this. A week in the same camp with her was more than a mortal man could be expected to stand. The reason I say that is I'd always heard that Clara's father and mother were separated. Well, they were separated all right. About a week earlier, I'd found out that Clara's father was in the state asylum where he'd been for the last twenty years and wasn't expected out any time soon. You notice I didn't say he was crazy. The thought had occurred to me that I might like to visit him and kind of check the place out for myself.

"Anyway, I'm drivin' along, and I got to thinkin' that a way to end a deer hunt real fast would be to get a deer real fast. Well, there weren't any zoos around that part of the country, so that was out. The old lady would probably know the difference between a deer and some farmer's holstein cow. There was always the possibility of a charge of cattle rustlin', too, but the thought of a year or so in jail compared to a week with Clara's mother wasn't botherin' me a whole lot. Still, there had to be a better way.

"There used to be a lot of coyotes in those mountains, and I finally decided that's what I would do. I'd shoot the first coyote I saw and get him skinned before the women saw him. Maybe I could tie a couple of branches to his head, just for effect, and convince them it was a real small deer. Of course, we'd haul the carcass home, and I'd have to eat a dead coyote, but I figgered I could do it.

"We got to the campsite and got ever'thing set up. By 'we' I mean Clara an' me. Her mother sat on a stump and gave orders. I'll bet I tore down that tent and moved it seventeen times.

"You know? ... there wasn't a deer or a coyote or any livin' thing besides us on that whole mountain. I know it for a fact, because I spent three days walkin' it while Clara's mother follered me around tellin' me how to do it.

"The nights were even worse. Clara's mother didn't snore ... she kind of snarled like a chainsaw cuttin' concrete. I'm tellin' you, the whole tent breathed when she did. I didn't sleep for three nights.

"On the fourth mornin' I either went to sleep or passed out along about daybreak. The next thing I know I'm bein' shaken awake.

'Luther,' says Clara, 'wake up. Mother's gone!'

"I sat up in bed. *Gone?*

'Yes, gone.'

"I started to smile. *Gone?*

24

'What if she's lost?'

"*Lost?* I was grinnin' now.

'Luther! Stop that! If you don't help me find mother, I'll never speak to you again. We're through! Do you hear me?'

"Well, I thought about it a while. Clara meant a lot to me, so I decided to go along. After all, lookin' don't mean findin' and lookin' for her mother is kinda like takin' a willow switch and goin' lookin' for tigers. You ain't gonna look real hard.

"So I pick up my gun and we start out. The sun is up so we can see good, but the brush and trees are thick, so we can't see very far. By an' by we come to a little clearing. Clara's mother is standin' out there, and she's eyeball to eyeball with a grizzly bear about twelve feet tall who stands loomin' over her.

"I just turned around and threw my gun over my shoulder and started back to camp. Clara grabbed my arm.

'Where are you going?' she yells.

"*Camp*, I reply.

'But what are we going to do?'

"*Nothin'*.

'Nothing?'

"*Sure*," I said. "*The stupid bear got himself into this mess. Let him get himself out.*"

"Well," says Luther as he drains his coffee cup, "I prob'ly wasn't cut out to be married anyhow."

26

You can make your own brass and copper cleaner by mixing equal parts of salt and flour. Add enough white vinegar to make a paste.

When I was a kid my dad had an old drinkin' buddy named Ira Brown. We didn't see Ira too often, but when he visited, it was a sure bet that he and dad would stay up late that night kneeling at the throne of Bacchus. (Bacchus was the God of wine according to the ancient Greeks.) Anyhow, they'd get belly-crawlin', grass-grabbin' drunk.

Now Ira was a mountain man who could disappear into the forest whenever he felt like it with nothing but his gun, a polk of salt and a ten-pound bag of cornmeal. A month or two later he'd turn up again, feeling mightily refreshed by his little separation from humanity. There's a good chance my brother and I were responsible in large part for those trips.

We weren't mean, of course, we were kind of creative ... so to speak. Ira never had kids (again, probably because of us) although he was married five or six times. He marched to a different drummer, and he never found a woman with good enough hearing, or imagination, to step to the same beat.

Actually, it's pretty remarkable that Ira was ever married at all. He wasn't what you would call handsome. Dad said that when Ira was a baby, he was so ugly his mother fed him with a slingshot.

His father had to tie a pork chop around the kid's neck just to get the dog to play with him.

As a young man Ira became a professional fighter. About half his fights were won before the first punch was thrown because he could out-ugly just about any boxer he came up against. He won most of the others, because he was big as a beer truck and he liked beating people up. There were times, though, when he got in the ring with somebody who was really good. As a result, when he was headed west, most of his nose pointed at the north star.

Well, Ira stopped by the house one evening, and the first thing he did was carry his bedroll into the back yard and roll it out. He never slept under a roof when he could avoid it. Then he went to his car, pulled out a quart of white lightnin' and followed Dad into the house.

Our back porch was at the corner of the house, and the roof extended to within six feet of the ground. Of course, you could enter from the side with plenty of clearance, but if someone was standing there, you had to walk around and, if you were tall, remember to duck. My brother and I always opened the evening's entertainment by standing at the side entrance so that Ira would have to walk around. He was tall, and he never remembered.

"Thunk!"

"Damn!"

Giggle, snicker, chortle — things were starting off well.

The rest of the evening wasn't so great, though. It was one of those times when Ira made us the butt of his jokes. It seemed like the more we tried to get the best of him, the more he made us look like fools. We needed to get even.

Someone had given us a goat. He was a big goat, kind of ornery, and, like goats are, he had a talent for walking on cars, getting into the garden, and making a general nuisance of himself. Not long before, he had pulled all the newly washed clothes off the line and brought several dark threats from my mother.

We roped the goat, tied him to a tree in the back yard and then watched to see how things were going inside. Dad and Ira sat at the kitchen table getting a little more pickled all the time. When they finally called a halt and agreed it was time for bed, Ira was barely in good enough shape to get there.

Before Ira left the house, we grabbed the goat, tied his feet together with a slipknot, and dragged him over to Ira's bed. Throwing back the quilts, we rolled in the goat, covered him up, and ran the rope over to some nearby bushes. We had barely taken cover when Ira lurched from the back door and groped his way through the dark to his bed.

Ira slept in nothing but his undershorts, and he was mumbling to himself as he disrobed. He got his boots off and his clothes piled to his satisfaction. Then he lifted the covers and crawled in.

I've concluded that there are three kinds of cussing. First there's the "Here I am at the store and the shopping list is at home" kind of cussing, which is really pretty mild. Then there's the "I've just mashed my thumb with the hammer" or "the neighbor has backed into my new car" type of cussing, which can get pretty colorful. Finally, there's the "I've just realized I'm in bed with a large, hairy animal" kind of cussing, which can make an Army drill sergeant blush. We jerked on the rope and turned the goat loose.

I guess I could tell you all about beds jumpin' around and the hollerin' and cussin', and quilts strung from here to yonder, but it probably isn't necessary. We kind of expected the lights in the house to come on, but when the nearest neighbor's house, a quarter mile away, lit up and then more beyond that, it didn't seem prudent to try to sneak back to our room. There was a lot of new, loose hay down in the barn, and we always did enjoy sleeping out.

Martha was stopped at a red light once and, just as it turned green, the engine died. While she was trying to get the car started, the guy behind her was leaning on his horn. Finally, she got out and walked back to the other car. "Let's trade places for a while," she said. "You try to get my car to start, and I'll stay here and blow your stupid horn."

That reminds me of a friend of mine named Larry who had something similar happen to him. It was back in the days when most cars had their hood latch in the grill. Anyhow, Larry gets stuck in a traffic jam, and the guy behind him lays on the horn until Larry can't take it any more. Now Larry's an ex-football player and big enough to make a small crowd all by himself. Larry gets out of his car and stands up ... and up ... and up. The other guy gets off his horn and kind of slides down in the seat. Larry walks to the front of the guy's car, pops the hood, reaches in and rips out the wires to the horn. When he slams the hood, the guy can't even be seen through the windshield.

A lot of people seem to think that if they protest loudly enough, things can only get better. Sometimes they're wrong.

Old Zeke has a long, white beard. I never bothered to ask him about it, because I figured he was just too lazy to shave. The other day he mentioned that he grew the beard when his kids started giving him neckties for his birthday. He claims they were so ugly he didn't want anybody to see them. Of course, that's not true.

Zeke is ninety years old now and about ten years ago, when a crony of his died, Zeke said he'd like to go to the funeral. Well, by the time the big day arrived, Zeke had forgotten about it. Some local folks stopped by and saw he wasn't ready. They got him dressed and put a necktie on him and went on their way. Zeke never showed up at the funeral. Later that day they found him sitting right where they'd left him. That necktie was the problem. Zeke thought he was tied to something, so he stayed right where he was.

I grew up out in the boondocks with a rifle in my hands and looked on the cost of a .22 shell as the price of a good supper. It wasn't much of a challenge to qualify as an "expert" rifleman when I went in the Army. When I got out of the service and went home, I found something really unusual. A lot of trees, fence posts, telephone poles and whatnot had little circles drawn on them, and there was a bullet hole smack-dab in the center of each one. Here was somebody who could outshoot me without half-trying. I asked around and ended up talking to a twelve-year old kid with a .22 rifle. I asked for a demonstration. The kid raised his gun, plugged a fence post and walked over to it. Then he pulled a crayon out of his pocket and drew a little circle around the bullet hole. A lot of people that we think of as better than we are, like that kid — well, just make sure they draw the bulls eye before they take the shot.

Some people complain about the bathing suits girls are wearing these days. I can't see what they're complaining about. I mean it. I <u>can't</u> <u>see</u> what their complaining about.

If you ever go clam digging, put your clams in a pan as soon as you can and cover them with water. Place the pan somewhere that you won't mind if it gets wet. Sprinkle corn meal over the water. The clams sense the food and start taking it in. Naturally, they have to expel water to do this, and most of the sand inside them is ejected.

It's more than beauty that lies in the eye of the beholder. When I was in the service, and I'd come home on leave, my mother would drag me around to visit every shirt-tail relative within a hundred miles. I especially disliked going to see Aunt Ida and Uncle Bob. Oh, they were nice enough folks and all that, but Aunt Ida was always trying to line me up with some nice girl. Aunt Ida always thought that my moral outlook was pretty bad anyway, and after spending some time in the Army, she figured it must be lower than a whale's naval. She was a woman on a mission.

We had no sooner walked in the door when she starts telling me about this wonderful girl that attends her church. "She's a beautiful girl," Aunt Ida says. "Refined and well-educated."

"Uh huh."

"She's an only child. Her family is quite wealthy."

"Uh huh. What else?"

"Well," Aunt Ida squirmed a little, "her father owns the plant where your Uncle Bob works."

"And ...?"

"Well ..."

"And ...?"

"Oh alright!" snapped Aunt Ida. "She is just a tiny bit pregnant."

Every parent thinks his kid is a genius. Every kid thinks his parents are idiots.

Around the restaurant, people are always leaving part of their cola, so I just pour it in a bucket. At night, before I go home, I dump it in the toilets and leave it until morning. It keeps the bowls clean. Kinda makes you wonder what the stuff does to your innards, doesn't it?

Once when our son Kyle was about eight or nine he brought home a report card that didn't look too good.

"Kyle," I said, "you can do better than this. Your pal Herbie Bennet gets grades a lot better than this."

"Sure he does," Kyle replied, "but that's because he's got a smart mom and dad."

Ol' Frank, the carpenter, is an admirer of corn products. He is especially fond of it in its most potent liquid form and always keeps a pint in the back pocket of his bib overalls. I've watched him walk the rafters of an unfinished barn just kind of leanin' one direction and then lurchin' off in another to where I just knew he was gonna fall and kill himself. Somehow he never has. A while back he was buildin' a barn for old man Barclay who's kind of stiff-necked about things like that. Frank had sort of half-climbed, half-fallen down a ladder and was standing there looking up at the roof. He pulled a bottle of ol' stumpblower from his pocket and took a jolt, not noticing Barclay standing nearby.

Barclay walked up to Frank, looked him right in the eye and said, "In all my years, liquor has never passed my lips."

Frank looked him over real slow and then put the cap back on his bottle, screwing it down extra tight. "You can bet it's not about to either," he said, as he slid the bottle into his hip pocket.

It was when I was just a kid that Jasper Hanks died. Jasper used to be quite a gambler. He hung out at the cardroom in the back of Jensen's Tavern. I guess all the smoke, late hours and cheap booze finally got to old Jasper, because one night down at Jensen's he just dropped out of his chair — deader'n a lawyer's conscience.

The other gamblers finally elected one of their group to go tell Bertha, Jasper's wife, that her husband had cashed in his chips for real this time. The man found Jasper's house and knocked on the door, trying to figure how to break the news. The door was jerked open and Bertha stuck her head out.

"What d'you want?" she demanded.

"Uh ..."

"Well, speak up. I ain't got all night."

"Uh ... are you the widow Hanks?"

"My name is Bertha Hanks, but I ain't no widow."

"I've got twenty bucks that says you are."

Well, Jasper was dead alright. The next day Charlie Parker, the caretaker at the cemetery, was digging his grave. Charlie had just had a fight with his wife, and he was thinking and digging, digging and thinking. Finally he threw his shovel out of the hole and started to crawl out. Charlie's a little fellow anyway, and he discovered he'd dug too deep and couldn't get out. Well, it got dark and the temperature was dropping, but as much as Charlie yelled, nobody came to help him. He was just about to give up when Cecil Burdette came along.

Cecil had a drinking buddy named Morton Boggs, and the two of them had been mourning Jasper's passing most of the day down at Jensen's Tavern. Cecil staggered up to the grave and peered into the hole.

"Help me out, Cecil," Charlie said. "It's late and I'm gettin' cold."

Cecil shook his head and gave a big sigh. "Well, gee whiz, Jasper, no wonder you're cold," he said. "They forgot to throw dirt on you. I'll go get Morton and we'll cover you up." He staggered away, ignoring Charlie's pleas for help.

It got pretty quiet for a while, and then someone just walked right up and fell into the grave. It was Morton. He didn't see Charlie. He just went to floundering around trying to climb out.

Charlie walked up behind him and said "It's no use Morton. You'll never get out."

But he did. Charlie said he made it with two or three feet to spare.

I put in a couple of handicapped parking spaces so the disabled folks could get into the cafe easier. About half the time those spaces are taken up by people who don't have so much as a bandaid on their finger. It used to really irritate me until I realized that those people honestly believe they're doing the right thing. They think those spaces are for the mentally handicapped as well.

Back in the days when people had good neighbors instead of good locks, the Fourth of July was quite an event. Mom spent the day before frying chicken, making potato salad and baking all kinds of great things to eat. Dad washed and serviced the car. He finished up by clamping a little American flag to each fender. Some people had flags with longer staffs that fit into little sockets on their front bumpers.

The morning of the Fourth, right after breakfast, the car would be packed with food, beer, soda pop and kids. Dad would crank 'er up, Mom would jump in beside him, and we were off! At some previously appointed spot we would meet all the neighbors from miles around, and the whole outfit would take off, caravan style, for a picnic spot in the mountains.

The day would be spent eating, drinking, telling stories and playing games. Our favorite game was one called "duck on the rock," and I'll get back to that shortly. The older kids had the standard-size firecrackers about like the ones you see today, even though it's illegal to sell them in most places. The little kids had "lady fingers"; a tiny little firecracker that went off with a 'snap' rather than a 'bang.'

As the day was drawing to a close, everybody packed up and headed toward home, but we all went to one family's house. There we all unloaded and continued on as before until it was completely dark. That was when the fireworks show began. The adults had brought along roman candles, pinwheels and even a few aerial bombs. It was a noisy, colorful and exciting way to end the holiday.

Now, back to "duck on the rock." It was a simple game, and all you needed were beer or pop cans and a large rock with a flat top. The person who started the game as "it" placed his "duck" (a pop or beer can) on the rock and stood by. A line was scratched in the dirt about twenty feet away and everyone else stood behind that line. To step over the line was to risk being tagged and becoming "it" yourself. Each person had a single can to throw at the "duck." In those days the cans were made of steel and had some heft to them. You could throw them pretty well. Hit or miss, you had to retrieve a can. However, the person who was "it" could only tag someone while the duck was on the rock.

The "duck" would often get knocked off the rock, and the person who was "it" would scramble to put it back on. He would be chasing after someone who had ventured over the line to retrieve a can when "CLANG!" — the duck would go sailing once again. He would have to race back and reset the "duck" before he could tag anyone.

On one Fourth of July the unthinkable happened. Everyone in the group had purchased their wetgoods in bottles. It looked like "duck on the rock" wouldn't be played that year.

Among our group was Milton Hewitt. Milt, along with his wife Claudia and their two kids, were long time members of the Fourth of July picnic party. Milt was a farmer and semi-professional drunk, who really enjoyed playing "duck on the rock." He was also one of those guys who gets happy and adventurous when they've had a few too many.

Late in the afternoon Milt lurched to his feet and announced that we would play "duck on the rock" after all.

"But we don't have any cans," someone said.

"We don't need cans," Milt replied. "All we need is one can to be the duck."

"But what will we throw at the duck?"

"We'll throw rocks."

Needless to say we kids thought it was a great idea. A pork and bean can was found to serve as the duck and the playing field was laid out in no time.

Now, who was going to be it? All the kids' mothers thought it was too dangerous for the children.

Milt scoffed at the idea. "I'll show you it's safe," he yelled. "I'll start off." He weaved his way over to the rock and sat the "duck" on it.

There was a herd of us kids, and we were ready. When I say that some of those kids had rocks, I don't mean pebbles. I mean <u>rocks</u>! Everybody from three to seventy-three was armed and ready. The game began.

Now, the adults were, for the most part, pretty careful. But the kids were just enthusiastic - and wild. At first Milt was hovering around the "duck," ready to reset it when it got hit, but pretty soon he was jumping around trying to avoid getting hit. He'd squall like a mashed cat when a two-pound boulder ricochetted off a shin and yell bloody murder when he got clipped up side the coconut with an egg-sized rock.

Actually, I found the whole thing to be an educational experience. A few years later when I read in my history books about people being stoned to death, I knew just what it looked like. So did Milt.

Now, the little kids with the big rocks tended to throw low. That's what hammered old Milt's shins. The smaller rocks flew high, and Milt's head and shoulders got peppered pretty well, too. When you consider there were about forty people chucking rocks, most of them kids, then you can understand what it must be like to face into a hailstorm of basalt and granite. But you had to give Milt credit. He was a "gamer" and even though he was yellin' and cussin', he hung in there and took his beatin' like a trooper.

I always liked Myrna Thompson. She was big as a yearlin' steer and every bit as strong, but she was usually pretty friendly and good natured. As a matter of fact, she was one of the people Milt really liked to play jokes on and kid around with. He'd been doing it all day.

Now I'm not going to say it wasn't an accident. On the other hand, Myrna was tall and athletic and could throw better than most men. I was standing right next to her, and she had a rock about the size of your fist. She drew back with that thing and cut loose a fastball that would have made a major league pitcher proud. It took old Milt right betwixt the runnin' lights, and he dropped like a poleaxed ox.

Everything got quiet, and we all kind of gathered around. Milt was wearing bib overalls, and when he went down his legs flew up in the air and his pant legs slid up. He had a crop of knots on his shins that would take all summer to harvest. It was kind of hard to tell about the rest of him until you got up to his head. His face looked like he'd been sortin' wildcats, and he seemed to be growin' a horn from between his eyebrows.

That ended the game. Claudia, Milt's wife, came by and poured beer on his head until he woke up. I guess you'd say that cured old Milt, and you'd be right. It was about ten hours later or around two in the morning when my folks woke up to a blood-curdling scream in their darkened bedroom. Milt jumped right in the middle of them, the bed slats broke, and they all wound up in a pile on the floor.

I didn't say it was a permanent cure.

Tom says that he and Alice got in a fight not long after they were married, so he went out by himself for a seven course Irish meal - a boiled potato and a six pack. That kind of got him started, and the next thing he knew, it was two a.m. He was sprawled on a park bench when a cop drove by. The cop stopped his car, got out and walked over to Tom. "What are you doing here at this hour?" the cop demanded.

Tom didn't say a word.

"Well, speak up," said the cop. "And it better be good."

"If it was that good," slurred Tom, "I'd be home tellin' it to my wife."

Speaking of the Irish reminds me of my Dad telling about his grandmother. "She was a little old back-haired, black-eyed Irishwoman from County Cork," Dad would say. "Sometimes my folks would leave me with her when they went someplace. Grandma would put me in a chair and say 'now you sit there and act smart.' It didn't take me long to discover that 'acting smart' meant that you don't do anything; you don't say anything; you don't even move if you can help it." Dad never said, but I presume it was alright to blink if he wasn't flagrant about it.

If that were to happen today, of course, all the adults involved would find themselves so far back in jail it would be necessary to shoot beans to 'em with a cannon. The government would take the kid and place him with someone who could provide a "meaningful parent-child relationship," which of course means that childish pranks like arson and ax murders, while not exactly prohibited, would bring a frown of parental disapproval. In extreme cases, this may even lead to a discussion centering on acceptable conduct as a reflection of societal concepts and morés versus these minor transgressions that may indicate a tendency toward antisocial behavior. The kid, of course, ain't required to listen.

Now don't get me wrong. I think child abuse is a terrible thing. But I also think that kids need rules and a certain amount of discipline to give structure and direction to their lives. It seems to me that too much discipline and none at all are both forms of child abuse. It probably wouldn't hurt any of us to "sit there and act smart" once in a while. We might learn something.

Sometimes you can't get as much attention with a yell as you can with a whisper.

Toothpaste works well to plug screw or nail holes in sheetrock walls. You can paint right over it.

Toby comes in for a meal now and then, and I always try to talk to him for a few minutes. For a while he lived not far from where Martha and I had our first house. Toby grew up the hard way.

It's true that he had both parents, but his father couldn't hold a job, and his mother never tried. Toby's dad had a hatred for the government in general and bureaucrats in particular. As a result, outside of some commodity food items, they never had government assistance.

Toby wore second-hand clothes and played with other kids' broken and cast off toys. But he was a bright little guy with blond hair and shining blue eyes. He did well in school, even though the other kids teased him about his clothes. His father looked on school as part of the government, and for

Toby to do well meant he was cooperating with them. Toby's progress was severely discouraged at home. The father thought he could have been somebody or done something important if he wasn't saddled with a kid. He could have been a mechanic, maybe even owned his own shop. It was all the kid's fault.

I was over at their house one day talking to his mother when Toby, who was in the second grade, came home from school. His birthday was only a few days away, and his mother had just told me she had bought two or three cheap toys for him.

"Mom," Toby asked shyly, "do you think I can have a cake for my birthday?"

"There's no money for that," his mother said.

"I won't get a present, will I?" he asked. But you could tell from the sound of his voice that he already knew the answer.

"We don't have money for things like that."

He bowed his head, and I could see him swallow hard before he looked up again, but his voice was steady and those big blue eyes were clear and trusting. "Could we wrap one or two of my old toys so I could have something to open on my birthday?"

"We're broke," his mother said. "We don't have any money to buy wrapping paper."

Toby only nodded and turned to go back outside. His mother looked up at me and smiled as if it were a great joke.

I've been in a war, and I've been a police officer. I've seen people die some pretty horrible deaths. Witnessing the death of wonder and innocence in a little boy's eyes is one of the worst things I've seen. Watching bright, shining hope turn to the dead ashes of hopelessness was more than I could take.

I'd talked to Toby quite a bit, and I knew the one thing he dreamed of was a bicycle. I went out that day and bought one. It was parked outside his door on his birthday.

Toby saw the bike and read the card. He opened his other gifts and played with them. Not once did he try to ride the bike. It was a week before he actually rode it around.

At first I was a little miffed about it all, but then I realized what had happened. The bike was a dream to Toby. He never thought he might actually have one of his own. Looking back now, I'm not sure he ever understood it was truly his.

Toby's folks moved soon after that, and I didn't see him for quite a few years. Not long ago, he told me he came home on his eighteenth birthday to find his few belongings shoved into paper bags and piled on the front step. He never went back.

Toby is almost thirty now, and he has lived in the same little three-room cottage for the last ten years. He works at a warehouse over in the industrial complex and comes home at night to sit with his dog at his feet and play his harmonica. He doesn't seem to want to have much to do with other people. I can't say I blame him.

I had a friend once who borrowed fifty dollars from me, and I haven't seen him since. After thinking it over, I've decided it was a pretty good investment.

College never did me any harm — until I had four kids who all wanted to go to college.

Ol' Zeke hobbles in to the restaurant every morning for a cup of coffee. Yesterday a businessman was here and got to talking to Zeke. When this fella found out Zeke was ninety years old, he said it was "incredible." Well, I've known Zeke all my life, and he doesn't move any slower than he ever did. Okay, maybe it's incredible that he's reached the age of ninety, but it took him ten years longer to get that old than it would anybody else.

It's never too late, no matter what you want to be or what you want to do. Tomorrow, next month, next year, they'll all come along anyway. Since you're going to be a day or month or year older anyhow, you may as well get started now.

I saw a lawyer the other day walking down the street with his hands in his pockets. I wish I'd had a camera. It's rare to see a lawyer with his hands in his own pockets.

Martha and I went to visit the Bennets the other day. When we walked by the kitchen window, we saw it was open. Tom and Alice's twelve-year old daughter Jane was doing the dishes. Martha said "Hi, Janie, is your mom home?" Janie's eyes narrowed and her mouth curled up in disgust. "What d'you think?"

Pete tells me he stopped by Ralph Ferguson's a year or so ago, and he drove in just as Ralph pulled up and took his golf clubs out of the car.

"That's it," Ralph said, "I'm never playing with Jack Flynn again."

"You two have a falling out?" asked Pete.

"Would you play with someone who picks up his ball and sneaks it out of the rough and back into the fairway?"

"Well ..."

"Would you play with someone who pretends to sneeze just as you're about to swing?"

"Well ..."

"Would you play with someone who cheats on his scorecard?" asked Ralph. "Would you?"

"Well, I sure wouldn't," said Pete.

"Uh huh," nodded Ralph. "Neither will Flynn."

Jensen got rousted out of bed by a phone call about six o'clock one morning.

It was Elmer. "What time do you open the tavern?" he asked.

"I open at noon, Elmer." Jensen went back to bed. He had just dropped off to sleep when the phone rang.

It was Elmer, only he sounded a little drunker than before. "When you open?"

"At noon, Elmer." Jensen slammed down the phone and went back to bed. Half an hour later the phone rang again. Jensen was boiling mad, and Elmer sounded like he was really plastered.

"What (burp) time (burp) open?"

"Look, Elmer," growled Jensen, "I open at noon, but if you'll leave me alone for a while, I'll come down at eleven and let you in."

"Not tryin' to get in," slurred Elmer, "tryin' to get out."

I must be getting old. I can recall when I could buy a car and have it paid for before the next election.

It isn't that I mind being a man of experience — it's just that it's not what I was lookin' for when I got it.

Frustration:	A teenage girl, a cordless phone and a home with a single bathroom.
"A minute":	Depends on which side of the door you're on.

On the whole, I'd say girls are easier to raise than boys. But with girls (ours at least), they reach a point when they're about fourteen or fifteen that they get meaner than a nest of rattlesnakes. It's at about that time in the kids' lives when you're afraid to go to sleep. One, because the boy isn't home yet and, two, because the girl is.

Tom has a boy in college.
"What's he going to be?" I asked.
"Well," said Tom, as he stroked his chin, "he'll be nineteen, if I decide to let him live."

I've got an uncle who's ninety-seven years old. The other day he told me he thought he was going to live a lot longer. He said he'd been reading the obituaries in the newspaper the last few months and almost nobody dies at ninety-seven.

Two boys came downstairs for breakfast and found their father sitting at the table. "What d'you want for breakfast?" he asked, as the kids sat down. "Oh, I dunno," the oldest one said. "I guess I'll have some more of them damned old cornflakes." "The father reached across the table and backhanded the kid off the chair. He turned to the younger one and asked "Well? What d'you want for breakfast?"

The kid looked down at his brother and then back at his father. "Well, I don't know," the kid said, "but you can bet your raggedy butt I don't want none of them damned old cornflakes!"

Bentonite is a super absorbent clay, often used in cat litter. Even if you don't have a cat, a bag of cat litter is handy to have around. The stuff absorbs moisture, bad odors and is fireproof. I use it to soak up oil on the garage floor. I drop a handful into the garbage can in case the liner leaks. In the refrigerator it picks up odors. Put it in the charcoal grill to catch fat drippings. It can be sprinkled on icy walks and steps for traction. The possibilities boggle the mind.

It seems to me that a lot of childhood problems could be easily taken care of if somebody was allowed to spank grandparents.

Old Barney was a moonshiner's horse. Except for the star on his forehead, he was a coal black gelding, high spirited and alert. If you were riding him along one of those twisting mountain roads, nobody would see you unless you wanted it that way.

Barney was born and raised in those mountains, and while other horses learned to pull a plow or work cattle, Barney learned how to transport moonshine.

The roads in those days were really just wagon tracks, and they rose and fell with the slopes, making sharp, blind turns at a creek or canyon or patch of boulders. Riding along, you might meet anyone at anytime, and they might be only yards away when you first saw them. It could be someone on a horse or in a buggy or car ... and it could be the sheriff.

But if you were riding Barney, nobody saw you. His ears were always moving as he listened for an unusual sound. When he heard something moving on the road, his training took over and Barney headed for the brush. Stepping carefully so he wouldn't break a stick or make any other noise, he'd slip off the road and work his way into a thicket and hide there. With his head and ears up, he'd stand watching the road until the traveller passed by. Then he'd return to the road and continue on as if nothing had happened.

If you were riding along and Barney suddenly headed for a place to hide out, all you had to do was rein him back into the road. He understood

then that it was permissible to continue on, and he would pass the other person without any problem. But the next person coming down that road wouldn't see you unless you wanted him to. Barney's first owner had trained him that way, because the guy was overly fond of his own product. Since it was hard to be sozzled and on the alert at the same time, he trained his horse to do it.

The years passed and Barney was sold to someone else. Horse trading, if not an occupation for most folks, was at least a hobby. Drinking, dancing, fighting and horse trading were the most popular forms of entertainment. After a while everybody in that stretch of the country had owned Barney at least once, some three or four times. Even in his twenties, he was still lively and alert even though his muzzle had gone grey with age.

Once my grandpa's brother Hal came into possession of a fine sorrel gelding. One front foot turned in a bit, but it was easily corrected if he was properly shod. He was only a three-year-old and still learning what was expected of him. Hal had the horse out in the front pasture and was working with him. When Hal looked up, he saw his brother, my grandpa, riding down the road on a snappy young black. Grandpa pulled up and they talked a while.

It took some time, but eventually the subject got around to horses in general and the two present in particular. Hal liked the young black that grandpa was riding. He was solid black, without a white hair on him and looked to be about an eight-year-old. Grandpa, on the other hand, liked the sorrel, even though the one hoof needed special care. Finally, they decided that the corrective shoeing on the sorrel made up for the few extra years on the black, and they switched saddles. Grandpa rode away on his new horse, and Hal turned the black into his corral. That night it rained.

When he walked out of the house the next morning, Hal thought he saw something odd in the corral. His new horse didn't look just right. He walked over for a closer look. The black now had a white star on his forehead, a muzzle grey with age and stoveblack dripping off his nose. It was old Barney.

In horse trading there is no mercy.

Every once in a while you run across someone who enjoys turning the screws on people. He really likes to make them sweat and suffer. And yet if the situation should be reversed, even for a little while, he can't handle it at all. Whether it's a crisis at the office or a leaky lifeboat with the food and water running out, you can bet someone else will be fed to the sharks.

Amy, one of the waitresses, says she likes working here because I'm fair. I told her that was nice to know.

"Yeah," she said, "you treat us all alike. Rotten."

"Talk like that could cut into your Christmas bonus," I said.

"Well," she smiled, "I found a couple empty beer cans on the way to work this morning. The deposit I'll get on them should just about make up for it."

One of these days I'm gonna have to go down in the basement and finish that dungeon I've been working on.

Actually this all goes back to a few months ago when Amy called in sick. I told her we'd all cover for her, and just as soon as I hung up, I'd get everybody together and see if anyone knew just what it was she did around here anyhow.

She was pretty sick and gone a couple of weeks. By the time she got back, she'd kind of forgotten our phone conversation. She thanked me again for covering for her. I told her we worked everything out. I just stood back there in the kitchen and talked to myself, and the customers all pitched in and talked to each other, and we didn't miss her at all.

You know, Amy is alright, but that girl can act downright surly sometimes.

Computers are like four-wheel drive vehicles - you can get stuck in places you never knew existed.

Committees are formed so that more people can share the credit with the one who does the work.

Martha and I raised two sons and two daughters, and I've come to the conclusion that trying to reason with a teenager is kind of like teaching a pig to sing. All it does is frustrate the teacher and irritate the pig.

I know I knock higher education from time to time, but I'm really all for it. What you get in college is the benefit of someone else's experience. If you look in the course catalog, you'll find the cost right there in black and white. Hopefully, along the way, you'll learn a little bit about yourself, too.

In the real world the cost of tuition is usually hidden among the figures in a contract or in the reason why you lost your job and your neighbor didn't. We all pay tuition.

I guess the reason I sit around trying to give good advice is that I'm too damned old to be a bad example.

I've never heard anyone successful attribute their prosperity to comfort and contentment.

Young Skip Mason stops by every once in a while. He turned twenty-one not long ago, and he'll never be any smarter in his life than he is right now. He's got a good job downtown, drives a new pickup and thinks anybody over forty has one foot in the grave.

Since he came of age, he's been spending a lot of time at Jensen's Tavern. I hear he's been something of a smart aleck and getting on the nerves of the older guys.

Well, there's a little room at the back of the tavern, and most people know better than to set foot in there, especially on Friday nights. That's when a few of the old farmers and ranchers meet for their weekly poker session. Last Friday night, Skip walked in there.

I had just opened up the cafe when Skip came in and sat down. "Well," I said, "I hear you're a poker player now." Skip looked like he had been run hard and put away wet.

"No," he said sorrowfully, "I'm not a poker player." He slowly shook his head. "But I can sure point out four ornery old devils that are."

Hey, I know you've got to go, but we're sure glad you stopped by. Remember, the coffee's always hot, and when you start back this way, hurry up ever' chance you get. Take care.

AUTHOR'S NOTE

Ever since I can remember, I've enjoyed talking to the old timers. They're just waiting to tell someone the stories of their youth, or the tales passed down by their parents and grandparents. If I talk to enough of them, I'm sure to hear a story now and again that is very much like one I've heard before. The people involved may change, or the circumstances might be somewhat different — even the punch line (if there is one) may be altered to some degree, but it's the same story. That's fine with me. There's always something different, even in a story I've heard before. Sauce, as they say, for the goose.

For example, there's the story of the time when the Army mechanized all its units and some animals were simply turned loose to wander away. A neophyte hunter went looking for a deer not long after that and bagged a big one. At the checkout station he couldn't wait to show the game officer the huge "mule deer" he'd taken. Naturally, the critter had long ears, shoes on its hooves, and a "U.S." branded on it. I've heard half a dozen people swear it happened right in their area.

The old timers have something to tell you. If you're not fortunate enough to have one in the family, or close at hand, then stop in at a nearby retirement home. Spend an hour a week if you can, but an hour a month or even an hour a year is something. And, believe me, you'll both be better for it.

GDT